Student Success Mindset

"The Ultimate Strategy Guide for Better Grades, A Winning Mindset, and More Enjoyable School Experience"

Student Success Mindset

"The Ultimate Strategy Guide for Better Grades, A Winning Mindset, and More Enjoyable School Experience"

Ariel Inspires

Copyright © 2020 Lion Press Publishing.
All rights reserved. No part of this publication may be reproduced, distributed, or transmitted in any form or by any means, including photocopying, recording, or other electronic or mechanical methods, without the prior written permission of the publisher, except in the case of brief quotations embodied in critical reviews and certain other noncommercial uses permitted by copyright law. For permission requests, write to the publisher, at the address below:

Attn: Book Coordinator
922 Peachtree Station Cir.
Peachtree City, GA 30269

Ordering Information:
Quantity sales. Special discounts are available on quantity purchases by corporations, associations, and others. For details, contact the publisher at the address above.
Orders by U.S. trade bookstores and wholesalers.

Connect with Ariel Inspires:
Website:
https://www.arielinspires.com/
https://www.arielmerch.com/

YouTube:
https://www.youtube.com/channel/UCaOsY_wcDjOdM5S8inxxeeA

Facebook:
https://m.facebook.com/ArielInspires/

Instagram:
https://www.instagram.com/arielinspires/
Twitter:
https://mobile.twitter.com/arielinspires

Email:
Info@arielinspires.com

ISBN
978-1-7351823-0-8

Dedication

To my wife and children for giving me inspiration every single day.

To the editing and design team, Sharee Moore and Dynasty Publishers, for all of your hard work.

Last but not least, to the person who lays eyes on this book and lays hold of the principles within.

I dedicate this to you.

Preface

I know what you're thinking, what is the student success mindset? Great question by the way. The student success mindset is a winner's attitude towards school and life. In this book you will learn different strategies, tips, and principles to help propel you towards student success. Keep it real, we all want to be successful in some capacity whether it be school, sports, or our professional career. I knew when I was in school I wanted to be successful, but I bottled it up and kept it to myself. I don't want that for you. That's what actually pushed me to write this book.

I know what you're thinking again. By now you're wondering, *Ariel, why should I listen to you?* Another great question by the way. Let me start by telling you my story.

I grew up in the small city of Syracuse, New York. I had no desire to get a good education. I just wanted to pass, make my parents proud, and not be a statistic. I had no motivation, I was insecure, and came from poverty. I grew up in the hood on government assistance such as food stamps and Section 8 Housing. No male in my family had any type of college degree. And I only had one aunt with a bachelor's degree.

During my senior year, I saw my friends selling drugs, dropping out, and going in and out of jail. One day, an officer in my school told me I was a good kid and one day he feared I would be dead or in jail for hanging with the wrong crowd or by being in the wrong place at the wrong time. That's when I realized I did not want to be a statistic. I wanted to be the first in my family to get a degree. Not only did I graduate high school, but I went on to get my associates degree from Genesee Community College and a bachelor's degree from one of the top schools in the country, Syracuse University. I've successfully built my company Ariel Inspires LLC, in which I do coaching, professional communication, and also operate a clothing brand. I travel the world doing what I love, whenever I'd love to do it.

The concepts, strategies, and principles in this book are based on my own experiences in the classroom and my reflections as an adult of what could have helped me if I had this information earlier on in life.

Feel free to highlight, underline, dog ear, doodle, or whatever you want in order to memorize the text in this book. This is your copy so make it unique to you. Use this book as a guide to help you navigate school and life. Dog ear your favorite chapter to refer back to it as often as you need. This book is your new accountability buddy, so pick it up when you need a little help, inspiration, or encouragement. Put it somewhere you can see it every day so it's not out of sight, out of mind. Put it next to the TV or video game or on top of your dresser. Whatever you decide, the choice is yours. Enjoy.

Time to be amazing.

Contents

Dedication *4*

Preface *5*

Introduction *12*
   Learned Limitations Activity **16**

Starting Point *18*

Healing Starts In the Mind *26*
   Gratitude Activity **30**

Actions Speak Louder than Words *32*
   Accountability Activity **36**

Character Development *39*

Honor Your Last Name *51*
   10 Reasons Why Activity **58**
   Question Activity **60**

Education = Opportunity 62
   Five Ways Activity 67

Take Inventory of Your Life 70
   Personal Inventory Activity 75

Start By Changing What You Can Control 77
   Reflection Activity 80

Student Success 83
   Student Success Definition Activity 89

Why = Power = Fuel 91
   Why Activity 96

Circle of Influence 98
   GPA Estimator Activity 112

Peer Pressure Awareness 114

Managing Expectations 121
   Expectation Activity 128

Balance and Rhythm 131

Time Management Activity	**136**
Goal Setting	*139*
S.M.A.R.T. Goal Activity	*160*
Study Habits	*162*
Bring It Home	*179*
Author Bio	*185*

Introduction

Welcome to the *Student Success Mindset*. This is the ultimate strategy guide for students like you, who are looking to get better grades, have a more enjoyable school experience, and develop a winning mindset to carry you to personal and academic excellence. I wrote this book to inspire students all across the globe to be the best student and the best person they could be. Not only is this book inspirational, but this book gives you the practical steps and strategies you need in order to succeed at being your best self.

This book was inspired by my past school experiences. In the past, as a student, I was often unmotivated, uninspired, and uninterested in being the best that I could be. I didn't try my hardest, I didn't give it my best effort, and I most certainly didn't shoot my best shot. I dragged my feet and ended up barely passing by the skin of my teeth.

I handed in assignments late, scrambled to get extra credit, and always looked to my classmates for help. I didn't have the strategies or mindset outlined in this book, and I didn't have anyone to help me develop the skills I needed in order to become my best self.

So, I decided to write this book in order to help students like you who are yearning to have that assistance to be successful, but are too afraid to reach out for help. This book will be one of the most important resources you come across in helping yourself get better grades, build better relationships, and help take control of your academic future.

I want to help aid in that process of going from:

- C student to an A student

- Unengaged to unlimited engagement
- Uninterested to uncontrollable thirst to be the best that you can be

Before we start – Be honest, is there anything in your life that is limiting you from being the best you can be? Is it money, age, intelligence, height, gender, religion, family, etc.? Give me your top 5 list of things you think are holding you back or limiting your life experiences. Name it and explain it. For example, if money is a current limitation, explain why below. This helps you become aware of some things you may have picked up in your lifetime. It also allows you to put it down if you outgrow it, or just choose to decide that you don't want it anymore. *Action cures all.*

So if money is limiting you, figure out how to save and make more. If your mindset/mentality is holding you back, watch YouTube videos on how to destroy limiting beliefs and build self-confidence. List it, explain it and then figure out what action you can take to cure it.

All students have the potential to push past learned limitations!

All the strategies and principles in this book not only apply to the academic world, but also to your life. We all know that one day you will stop going to school, but you will never stop learning. I want to give you the strategies that are transferable in your personal, academic, and professional life because what's better than being a great student?

… Being a great person!

Learned Limitations Activity

List your top 5 limiting beliefs and why you think they are limiting you. Bonus, list how you can solve them.

_____

_____

_____

_____

_____

_____

_____

_____

_____

_____

Starting Point

Your starting point for student success is hidden in plain sight. It's so simple to point out, that it is grossly overlooked. It's so easy to identify, that some people actually have a hard time believing it could be so simple. The simple things in life are sometimes the most difficult to believe.

I know you're asking, "Well where do I start?" It's a legit question. Where do you start? Do you start on the moon? Nah, that wouldn't be right! That's not a good starting point unless you have the science and technology to sustain yourself on the moon lol, and even if we did it still wouldn't be the best answer.

Do you start with your parents? Another good answer but not the answer we are looking for because we can't control the actions of our parents. Don't you agree? yes or no? Cool, good to know. So, to answer your question ... you start within yourself. You start with your thoughts and actions. Why? Because that's what you can control first and foremost.

There are two main things we control in life and that's attitude and effort. There are things in our lives that we can control and there are things in our lives we cannot control. We cannot control where we were born, the family we were born into, or the environment we inherit from birth. Think of life as a game of UNO. When we play UNO, we get dealt a certain number of cards. After all the cards are dealt, we cannot go through the deck and exchange cards, we cannot add or take away cards and neither can we give our cards up or swap them.

We must play the cards we are dealt! No ifs, ands or buts about it. Complaining won't change anything, whining will not change anything and neither will crying. It might get you a little sympathy, but it won't get you success. Again, we have to play the cards we are dealt and we might not like it, but guess what? We can win with them! We can succeed with them. We can accomplish our wildest dreams with the cards we are dealt.

Throughout this book we will piece together how we can do this. I'm not here to give you any mumbo jumbo or fairy tales. No cap. No games. No fakery. No luck. Just practical strategies and principles I used to help change my life. These strategies and principles have withstood the test of time. They not only worked for me but they worked for many people throughout history who applied them as well.

I started life in a single parent household of six. It was me, my mom and my five other brothers and sisters. I didn't live with my dad growing up. I always knew my dad, but it was my mom who raised us. I grew up in an unstable household. I lived in two states and four cities. I wasn't a military brat, but we moved around a good bit. More than the average person for sure.

My mom was a runner. So, every time she had a major problem she ran, and everywhere she ran, she took us with her. We lived in Albany, NY; Rensselaer, NY; Syracuse, NY and Philadelphia, PA. We grew up on social services, government assistance, food stamps, public assistance, and Section 8. We grew up poor but my mom did a great job at masking our poverty.

I didn't realize we were poor until I was late into my high school years. We had it great from time-to-time as I can remember. It wasn't always hard for sure. There were some great times sprinkled in there. It just got worse as I got older. However, that didn't stop me from graduating. I played the cards I was dealt and of course I complained, I whined and cried about it at first. Over time, I realized there were kids who had it just as bad as me, or worse. I realized I was getting the same education as the kids in my school and in my neighborhood. We all got on the same bus and learned from the same teachers in the same classroom. I didn't notice any difference in our opportunities.

So, what was there to complain about? In my immediate reality we were all on a level playing field. I had my issues and I had my fair share of family and friend drama. But guess what? So, did everyone else. I wasn't the only one. I had brothers and sisters and friends. I saw that they were going through things too.

How was I supposed to know what the neighbors were going through? How was I supposed to know what my cousins were going through? Or the people I shared a hallway with? What about the administrators and the teachers ... they are human too, right? They have to eat. They have to travel. They have problems and they get sick.

Just like me. Just like you. Just like all of us. We are all human at the end of the day and we have to be mindful of that. We should always take that into consideration. Maybe every now and again we should step back out of our own mind and put ourselves in the minds of others for a change.

This helps us get a better perspective. It helps us gain a better overall understanding. And it allows us to empathize and feel compassion for ourselves and those around us. Whether we like it or not, we share this world and we share our communities, grocery stores, malls, schools, and everything else.

I learned this the hard way. It took me way too long to acknowledge this fact. And I don't want that for you. I want you to get this understanding sooner rather than later. I want you to acknowledge the situation in its complete context. I don't want you missing out because you overlooked the context clues.

Let me share a story with you. There was a man who said, "If 5 years ago, I knew the information I know now, my life would be set." There was a 40-year-old man who said, "If 20 years ago, I had access to the things I have now, my life would be set." Then there came a wise man who said, "With the information and resources I have now, in 5 years my life will be set."

What's going on here? The first two people in the story felt regret for their current situation. They both imagined what life could have been if they had this information or the resources earlier. But the wise man was different. He could have said the same thing as the two previous men, but he didn't.

He said he is going to take the information and resources he has now and he will make his situation better. He will make it different. The wise man had a different perspective. He didn't look to the past, but he focused solely on the opportunities he has now. He focused on the future.

We can learn from the wise man. We can also learn from the other men. We can choose to look back and regret what we didn't do, what we could have or should have done, and what we didn't have. Or, we can take what we have now and use it to our advantage. We can choose either/or. That's our own right. But me, I'll choose to think as the wise man.

Healing Starts In the Mind

Healing starts in the mind, guess what else starts in the mind? Belief. Belief starts in the mind. We as humans do nothing without belief. We pass and fail based on our beliefs. We do what we believe we can do.

If you believe you will fail the test, 9 times out of 10 you will do what it takes to fail the test. What does it take to fail the test? Not studying, not reading, not paying attention in class, not going to school, and not caring about failing. If you believe you will pass the test 9 times out of 10 you will do whatever it takes to pass the test. You will study, read, pay attention, get to class on time, and get a tutor if need be.

We change our grades by changing our minds. We change our lives by changing our minds first. Guess what? Changing your mind is free. It doesn't cost you one rusty penny. Changing your mind is solely and entirely up to you. You are the master of your mind. You are the leader and sole owner of your mind.

You own it and control it. So, make good decisions with and for it. Take good care of it, guard it, feed it, protect it, nurture it. Most importantly, don't give it to anyone else. Not friends, not family, and most definitely not social media. You only get one mind, so don't waste it. You know the old saying, "A good mind is a terrible thing to waste." I couldn't agree with this quote more. It's reached its maximum degree of agreeability. If that is a thing, lol.

I remember when I was in high school and basketball tryouts were coming around. I believed I couldn't make the team. I had convinced myself I wasn't good enough because I was new to the school, I didn't know anyone, and the coach had favoritism amongst the players he was familiar with.

I didn't even attempt to go to tryouts. My hoop dreams were over before they ever got started. Why? Was it because I didn't have my mom's support? Nope, I had her support. Was it because my dad didn't believe in me? Nope, he believed in me. So, what was it? It was my lack of belief in myself.

I had no confidence, low self-esteem, and a ton of insecurities. But mainly it was a lack of faith. Now if I believed in myself, does that mean I would have automatically made the team? Of course not. It's deeper than that. Belief is only the first step in the equation. It's the starting point. Not the end point. Your belief has to be backed by actions.

Heal the mind and your life will follow. Think *I can*, do not think *I cannot*. Think positive thoughts and do not think negative ones. Continue to be optimistic and do not allow the world around you to make you pessimistic. Look on the bright side, find the good. It's so easy to find the dark side and point out the flaws in everything.

Gratitude Activity

Every morning and every night try finding the good in the day. This is a simple mindset shift to ignite change in your life. Find something to be grateful for. Count your blessings. Be grateful for the fact you woke up this morning, the fact you made it this far, for your friends and family. Now you try. What are you grateful for?

_____

_____

_____

_____

_____

_____

_____

_____

HEALING STARTS IN THE MIND

Actions Speak Louder than Words

The secret recipe for success is actually not a secret. It's widely known throughout the earth. But saying the word *secret* makes success sound cooler. It's more mysterious, and as humans, we are naturally curious. So, if someone has a secret we want to know it. Dang, we so nosey, lol.

Anyway, back your belief with your actions. Let your *words* be backed by your *works*. People will take you way more seriously when you show them better than you could tell them. I can tell you I will be an A student all day, but my words mean nothing when my test grades come back and they're all F's.

"Don't allow your mouth to write a check your actions can't cash." Don't talk a good game knowing you can't back it up. Don't tell me you're going to get all A's when you know dang well you are a C student. Having high standards are great, but having a realistic grip on your situation is even better. Start slow and work your way up. Remember, it's the tortoise who wins the race, not the hare. Slow and steady my friend. Slow and steady.

Give yourself time to be a beginner. Give yourself time to develop good habits. New habits erase bad habits or you can substitute/swap habits. Allow yourself the permission to fail and try again. Allow yourself time to try new things. For example, get a tutor, start a study group, read the chapter, then read it again, take notes, and quiz yourself.

Don't rush the process, trust the process. It's not a sprint but a marathon! This is not a race of life. Again, say it with me, it's not a race. You are not in competition with anyone. Get out of that mentality as soon as you possibly can. That mindset/attitude is counterproductive to your overall happiness and academic success.

I used to measure myself up against everyone in my class. As long as I wasn't last I was good. I set the bar so low and what was worse is – I reached it! I was naturally talented enough to barely pass without studying. So, I mistakenly thought I was better than the kids who dropped out, got a lower grade than me, or who were failing.

But I didn't realize I was putting myself through major self-sabotage. Trying not to be last is no way to win at life. It's no way to become happy and it's definitely not a way to be successful. When you're trying to not be last, you give very little effort. It's like you don't even try. If you don't challenge yourself, if you don't push yourself and if you don't hold yourself accountable, no one else will either. That's the number one formula for failure and living a life below average.

The greats push themselves past their limits. The successful people challenge themselves to be better than they were last marking period, last year, and who they were yesterday. Winners hold themselves accountable.

They don't wait for teachers, coaches, administrators, and parents to do it. They have high standards for themselves and they push themselves harder than anyone could. They raise the bar high and every time they reach it, they aim it higher.

Accountability Activity

Give me three areas in your life where you can hold yourself more accountable. For example can you hold yourself more accountable with being to school on time, keeping up with your chores or workouts? List the reasons why. Would working out more help you be a better athlete? Would doing your chores on time make your parents proud? Lastly, write how this would have an impact in your life. Would it make you happier? Would it help you make more money? Would it help you get better grades?

_____

_____

_____

_____

_____

_____

_____

ACTIONS SPEAK LOUDER THAN WORDS

Character Development

Character development, when is the last time you heard someone talk about developing their character? Growing up, I never talked about developing my character. My friends or family never talked about developing their character either. It wasn't important to us because it was one of those out of sight, out of mind kind of things. Character consists of the intangibles. The intangibles are the things we can't touch or grasp physically but we can see it in action. For example, responsibility, self-confidence, leadership, and drive are all intangible. We can't touch it. I mean I never touched or grasped self-confidence with my hands or feet, but I have felt confidence in myself when I studied for a test and I quizzed myself prior to the test with flashcards. That exercise of quizzing myself really helped boost my confidence. I felt so prepared and ready for that test.

I couldn't go to the store and buy self-confidence. I couldn't find self-confidence in my closet or under my bed. I had to develop it, I had to train for it, I had to do something in order to receive it. Character development is one of the most important aspects to get a grip on in order to be the best that you can be. Being responsible is another highly sought after characteristic. Why? Because people who are responsible are trustworthy. They can be relied upon to remember very important information and be trusted to handle very important tasks. Responsibility is another intangible characteristic that can't be packaged in a box. It can't be found outside under a rock neither can you buy it in a store or online. Responsibility is something that is learned over time, it comes with maturity.

The older you get, the more responsible you become for your actions and thoughts. As children, we don't understand the concept of responsibility. We are very carefree because we are so young and undeveloped. We don't know much and we don't care to know much. As children, all we want to do is play and have fun. As we get older and our brains, body, and mentality develop, we start to see life differently and value different things. Responsibility is one of the more desired character traits because it's hard to be responsible and take accountability for your actions.

When looking for companionship, or even employment, people like to be around responsible people and bosses like to hire responsible people. The more responsible you are, the more likely you are to get a promotion, be trusted to take on harder tasks, and make more money. Even when looking for a life partner, people like to marry responsible people because they know when they marry someone they want to know they will be responsible for trusting their life with that person. That's a lot of responsibility that comes with being an adult. You have to get a job or create a job and take care of children if you choose to have them. Also, you're responsible for all of your actions. No longer can you blame your parents for your mistakes and mess ups. It's mainly on you as an adult.

Can I ask you a question? Is character development important to you? Be honest, this is a judgement free zone. If it isn't already, right now is the best time to make it important to you. Why? Because character is the foundation for a successful life. Will developing your character make you stress-free in life? No, nothing can take away the stressors and pressures of life. But will developing your character help you relieve the stress in your life? Of course, it will. Having good character helps you manage your problems better. Stress is related to the level of problems you have in your life. The bigger the problem, the larger the stress levels.

How can you develop your ability to handle and manage problems? Responsible adults devise a plan and stick to it. So, if you have a problem, your intangible characteristics come into play and help you put together a plan. Once you put together the plan, you shrink your problems down to size and make them easier to handle. They no longer are mental monsters trying to frustrate and deter you. They become little mental ants easy to crush. Planning is another intangible characteristic that successful people develop and know how to use, when necessary. Characteristics are sometimes what separates job applicants from each other.

For example, there are two people going for job interviews. Both have master's degrees, both have 5 years of prior job experience, and both have really good references. So, who gets the job? The candidate with the better intangibles of course. The person with the better characteristics and personality. The candidate that displays responsibility, self-confidence, trust, leadership, and accountability. All these character traits, and more, are very important to develop early in life. The earlier these things mean something to us, the earlier chance we have at becoming successful.

Don't get me wrong, being immature and irresponsible to a certain extent, are definitely more popular in high school and college. When I was in school, girls liked the bad boy and guys found the loud girl more attractive. The bad boy who skips class, gets in trouble, and barely passes is way cooler than the quiet, shy, guy who passes all his classes. The girl who was loud, putting herself out there, seeking attention and dressing with less clothes got more attention than the quiet, reserved girl who kept to herself. Not saying these characteristics are bad, I'm not here to judge anyone. It's just during the time when I was in school, these were the norms. Developing good character wasn't on the forefront of our important life decisions list, although it should have been.

Developing good character in school leads to opportunity, as well. When I was in junior college I was a good student. I went to class on time, all the time and I was respectful to my teachers and friends. I also developed a positive rapport with Mrs. Martin, the associate dean of student support services. She became my campus angel.

One night, out of sheer boredom and ignorance, my friend brought fire crackers to my dorm. They were M 80s. They made a big bang and they were loud and illegal. We weren't aware of it at the time. Or at least I wasn't. So, a group of us were really bored late at night around midnight. We all decided to light them in the parking lot. So, without any thought or plans we watched them do it. At the time, we thought it was harmless fun. Then campus security called the police on us.

They didn't catch us in the act but they definitely had all five of us on camera. The cops came and brought the K-9 dogs. They searched our dorm for the fireworks, but they didn't find anything because we hid them perfectly. Later that week, after the campus authorities found out, our family found out, and the school administrators found out, they handed down punishments. Three of my friends were kicked off the campus.

My friend and I went to court and were sentenced to community service. My friend and I were not the ones handling the fireworks, but we were guilty by association. I was saved also because of my character. My personality and relationship with the school saved me from being kicked out entirely. I had a good reputation with the dean of students who went to bat for me against the rest of the board. She put her reputation on the line because she believed in me and who I was. She knew it was an honest mistake and we didn't hurt anyone. We were just bored college students who made a bad decision. If I would have never developed my character and developed my relationship with the dean, only God knows where I would be right now.

How do you develop good character? Start by being more responsible in your house. Keep your room clean, do your chores on time or ahead of time. Take on more responsibility by picking up more chores from someone else or doing extra elsewhere. Get to school on time or early. This develops accountability. Start planning your days, weeks, months and years. This develops forward thinking and looking ahead, as well as preparation. Schedule your activities from study, to sports, to TV, and sleep. Wake up early, it will give you more time to work out, read, and do homework. Develop initiative by doing responsible things without an adult having to tell you. Develop good decision-making habits such as thinking things over critically, listing the pros and cons and taking time to make big decisions without rushing. I always lead with, "Let me think about it before I give someone a decision."

I like to say, "Please allow me 24 hours to get back to you." I will say I need 72 hours, if it's a really big decision. I also like to say, "Let me check my calendar and I'll get back to you." Decision making and critically analyzing situations is a very profitable skill to develop. All-in-all, developing good character starts and ends with your thoughts and actions. Choose this day to change the way you think about character development. Choose this day to start acting differently. Act more responsible, act more mature, act like you have been here before. Let me paint a mind picture for you. In football, imagine how it looks when a player scores a touchdown and they act like they never scored before. They celebrate in a way that makes the other players look bad. They do things that can be seen as showing up their opponent and making them feel and look bad. They behave like they have never been there before and will never score again.

It's usually the guys who rarely score who act like that. It's usually the guy with no class who acts like that. It's usually the guy who is immature who acts like that. But the professionals, the guys with high standards, the guys who score a lot – They don't act like that. They don't show their opponent up. They don't act classless. They keep it clean and professional at all times. Why? Because they act like they have been there before. Have you ever gone to a restaurant, a gym, an amusement park and little kids are acting up? They can't sit still, they can't be patient, and they are misusing or messing something up. Why? Maybe it's because they haven't been there before and they don't know the rules or the standards.

You can see in their behavior they are not sure what's going on. Because they haven't been there before, they don't know any better. It's not their fault, we all make mistakes. As they get older and more informed, they will do better. So, it's up to you to be a good role model and set the example of class, professionalism, and good character. Act like you have been there before even if you haven't. Act like it. I was in the hood, the ghetto and lived in poverty. But when I went to school and work I didn't act like it. I acted differently. I acted mature, I acted like I had a lot of sense because we all do. We all have a lot of sense. Let's not doubt ourselves or undervalue our character and intelligence.

Honor Your Last Name

While traveling from school-to-school and talking to different students, I became aware that the majority of the student body lacked motivation. Their focus was on money, fashion, material things and partying. Of course, all those things are cool in a specific context. Everybody likes to have fun and hang out, myself included. When deciding what to do when having fun, I think about my last name. Why my last name? I think about my last name because I always keep my legacy on my mind. My legacy is attached to my last name. My last name is attached to my legacy. My last name is attached to my children, my wife, and my family. My last name means a lot to me. My legacy means a lot to me and over time, I found that whenever I feel a lack of motivation or feel down and out, I think about honoring my last name.

Bringing honor to your last name is super important. Why? Because your last name goes everywhere you go. Have you ever heard the quote "your reputation precedes you?" That means that before you walk into the room, a person has already heard something about you that can be good or bad. Bringing honor to your last name ensures that you are doing everything you can do to build a good reputation for yourself. In school, in the home, or on the job you should try your best to make a good impression and leave that place with a pleasant experience. When I was a freshman in high school, my character wasn't important. My last name? Who cares? I was not worried about being a good person or making a good first impression.

It had a direct impact on my attitude toward life and myself. It affected me, mentally, emotionally, and physically. I didn't care about anything. I had a careless attitude. You thought I was so mean? So what? You thought I was a bad guy? So what? You thought I didn't care and was selfish? So what? I was immature, irresponsible, and insensitive towards others. This made people look at me funny, not want to be my friend, or gave people a reason to not care about me or help me out in my time of need. I was lonely and in a dark place yet no one could see or hear my cry for attention.

Except there was this one teacher, Mrs. Daviau. She spoke life into me when I wasn't aware of my greatness. She saw potential in me from the start. She believed in me and, most importantly, she not only *told* me but she *showed* me. She didn't see me as who I was. She saw me as who I was going to be. She saw me passing 10th and 11th grade English. She was both my 10th and 11th grade English teacher because I failed 10th grade English, so I had to take both that year. She motivated me and she put up with me. She gave me a lot of chances. Too many chances. There would be days where I would be acting up in class, trying to make people laugh, showing up late and not doing my work. She would rarely ever kick me out. She would be really patient and polite to me. She wouldn't yell, or get mad sometimes she even joked with me. I was really surprised by the way she treated me because it wasn't normal; it wasn't what I expected.

Over time, she got to know more about me and I learned more about her, as well. I started to see her as a person and not just a teacher. She was like a friend-teacher. A teacher who is really cool, like a friend. She was nice to everybody, but I feel like she was super lenient towards me. When we had catch up days or slow days in class, she allowed my girlfriend to come to class with me because my girlfriend was in study hall. She knew my girlfriend was really nice and would keep me in place. She would babysit me so Mrs. Daviau could help the other kids. I thought that was so amazing.

I devoted that year to really applying myself and being extra studious in school. That experience helped me to understand the importance of being a good student and person. When people like you and you do good by them they treat you nicer and go above and beyond for you. She showed me that, and in return, I wanted to show her I could pass, I could be a good student and I could change the reputation I created for myself. It's never too late to bring honor to your last name. it's never too late to change your behavior. It's never too early or too late to become a better student or person. You don't need anyone's permission to change. You just need a reason. Lots of reasons. The more reasons, the better. She gave me a reason to do well. She helped me see school differently and she helped me believe in myself and honor my last name.

You can change and don't need your friend's permission, society's opinion, or the acceptance of anyone on social media. You can start to bring honor to your last name by changing your decisions. We are made up of the sum total of the decisions we make.

Make good decisions that will benefit you today and tomorrow. A mentor told me to do something that will help me earn money today and plant a money seed for tomorrow. That takes care of my present and my future. Take that same concept and apply it to your last name and character. Is what I am doing right now bringing honor to my last name today and tomorrow? Will this decision bring honor or dishonor to my last name? Is this a good look or a bad look? Will this help me be a better person, or would people look at me negatively? Is this the best way to get the job done, or is there a safer and more efficient way that I am not aware of?

Don't stress, this takes time. The good thing is the earlier you start the faster you will get better at doing it. This is a lifelong practice and skill that will help you make better decisions, be a good person, and bring honor to your last name.

10 Reasons Why Activity

In this exercise you'll train yourself to have more reasons to do better, than excuses not to do better. Write 10 reasons why you should be a better student in the space below.

_____

_____

_____

_____

_____

_____

_____

_____

_____

_____

HONOR YOUR LAST NAME

Question Activity

Circle Yes or No to the questions below. If you circled No to any of the questions, use the space below to explain how you can make a commitment to making better decisions.

Have you made a decision to be a good student? (Y/N)

Have you made a decision to be on time to class? (Y/N)

Have you made a decision to be nice to others when they are not nice to you? (Y/N)

Have you made a decision to study no matter if you feel like it or not? (Y/N)

Have you made a decision to give school all your energy and might? (Y/N)

Have you made a decision to get better grades? (Y/N)

Have you made a decision to be a better son or daughter? (Y/N)

Have you made a decision to be a better friend? (Y/N)

Have you made a decision to physically workout more often? (Y/N)

Have you made a decision to join a club? (Y/N)

Have you made a decision to volunteer? (Y/N)

Have you made a decision to save money? (Y/N)

Have you made a decision to read more books? (Y/N)

Have you made a decision to make curfew on time? (Y/N)

Education = Opportunity

Most students think school is not important. Better yet they believe some of the subjects they are learning are pointless. I wouldn't say they are pointless. The objective is to create well-rounded individuals. That means we will have to learn some information we won't use immediately, maybe we may never use the information. That may be 100 percent true. Here's the thing. As I get older, and talk to older people, one common theme I notice is we always learn some information that we don't use. I have read so many books and articles. I read so many pamphlets for work. I took multiple online courses and there is no way I will remember it all or use it all. That's not the point.

The point is to learn and grasp the information whether I like it or not. The point isn't to either like it, or not like it. You just have to learn how to understand it, use it on the test, display that understanding, and keep it moving. Don't allow the excuse, "When will I ever use this?" to make you have a bad attitude towards school. The information you learn in school is very important to life. School unconsciously and consciously teaches you way more useful information then non-useful information. For example, school teaches discipline, networking, good manners, time management, sacrifice, commitment, responsibility, compassion, empathy, toughness, and a bunch of other intangibles.

How does school teach discipline? It teaches you how to get up early and make it to school on time. That's discipline you can use when applying for a job because you will have developed years of experience with being early. How does school teach responsibility?

Handing in your homework on time is being responsible. How does school teach sacrifice? When you have to decide whether to study or play your video game. Whether to go to class or skip it, get pizza or salad. Those are all minor sacrifices. You're giving up something in exchange for something or someone else. That's a sacrifice. How does school teach toughness? When you have to battle to get good grades. When you have to develop tough skin and when kids are picking on you. When you have to stand up for yourself and when someone is accusing you of doing something wrong. Those are all occasions that could require you to be tough.

Education equals opportunity when it comes to getting and creating a job. Education equals opportunity when it comes to knowing right from wrong. Education equals opportunity because the more you know, the more valuable you are. The more you know, the more problems you can solve. There's a great analogy that goes something like this. There was a factory and the equipment in the factory started to break down. No one in the factory knew what to do so they called the manager. The manager came down and he couldn't solve the problem either. After hours of trying things, thinking and deliberating on what to do, they called in professional help.

When the professional got there, he looked at the machine for 10 minutes. Then he said, "I know what to do." He went in and turned one screw. After turning the screw and starting up the machine, everything worked good as new. The manager was shocked and so happy. Then the professional handed him the bill. It read, turning the screw equals $1. Knowing what screw to turn equals $9,999! The manager was lost for words. He was flabbergasted. Moral of the story is this: Being an expert in a certain field of study gets you paid more. This story demonstrates the difference between knowledge and action, in this case knowledge was more important. Action is important, knowing where to apply the action makes the difference.

The common understanding is that knowledge is power. But in its true essence, applied knowledge is power. Information without application leads to frustration. It does you no good to know and not do. The benefit comes when you know *and* do.

Education equals opportunity because when you have the education, or information, or knowledge you can qualify for different jobs. Also, if you do not get the job you desire, you can take your information and create the job you desire. The potential is endless when you take knowledge and use it to your advantage. But here is the thing: we have to acquire the knowledge. We can't look at getting an education as pointless. That's a bad perspective. We must be life-long learners. Always be willing to learn new things whether you use it one time or a thousand times. The more you learn, the more you earn.

Five Ways Activity

Try this exercise. Give me five ways in which school is beneficial to you unconsciously and consciously and explain why. I bet you didn't even know you were learning when you were just going through your day-to-day unaware of all the benefits of school. For example, school consciously teaches you history, math and social studies. **School unconsciously teaches you _____.**

_____

_____

_____

_____

_____

_____

_____

EDUCATION = OPPORTUNITY

Take Inventory of Your Life

So, here is something I wasn't taught in school and that is to take inventory of my life resources. This strategy has had a huge impact on my life and will have that same impact on yours, if you use it. It's as simple as it sounds.

In order to assist you on your journey, start taking inventory of the people and talents you possess. This will help you use them to your advantage when the time is right. Taking inventory also helps you gain clarity on where and who to start with. This allows you to become more aware of who you can trust and lean on in times of need. You'll also straighten out the list of people who are of no benefit to you. It's your own personal network.

You already know you have yourself, which is your will power, but what are your gifts and talents? What are you good at? What are you not good at?

Now you are going to list out your talents and the people in your corner. For example, my talents are communication, energy, planning, leading, and work ethic. The people who I could turn to for help were my mom, my girlfriend at the time, and Mrs. Daviau, my 10th and 11th grade English teacher. I had no tutor, no coach, no mentor, and my high school guidance counselor was too busy to ever be of any real help. Luckily, when I got to college my academic advisors were always there for me. They were in my corner the most.

Now you have to take inventory of your gifts. Who can you turn to for help? Keep in mind, that when taking inventory, don't include all your friends. Why? Because for the most part, you are already aware of them and what they can do for you. This exercise is to help make you aware of some people in your life who are older and more experienced.

Think about someone in your family, maybe someone you trust in your school or neighborhood. Check your phone's contact list and check your social media pages for possible people who can lend you some advice or help you out in tough situations.

I know what you are thinking. *I don't have any skills or talents*. But you do. We all do. Most of us just aren't aware of our skills and talents because we have been suppressing them in order to fit into society, our family, or our friend groups. This happens naturally because, as humans, we want to fit in. We want to feel like we are a part of something. We want to get along and be involved in what's going on. We all want to be in the loop or be in the know.

Very rarely, do we want to stand out or be different because in school we are often mocked for sticking out. We are made fun of for our gifts, talents, and skills. The very smart kid is called a nerd, the tall kid is called a giraffe, and the kid who is always answering the questions is called a teacher's pet or goody-goody two shoes.

People are cruel and bullying is a real thing. But all-in-all, you have a skill, a talent, and/or a gift. If you don't know what it is - congratulations - you win the day because you get to discover your gift. Discovering new things is always celebrated. Like when you find your phone after you misplace it or when you learn new information. New discoveries are an exciting time and today you get to discover your uniqueness.

It could be anything from communication skills, to charisma, charm, humor, ability to have fun, outgoing personality, physical fitness, organization skills, good memory, you follow directions well, good listening skills, leadership ability, toughness, confidence, outspokenness, fast learning ability, or creativity, just to name a few. Take some time to think about your unique skills and figure yourself out, or at least narrow it down to your top three.

Ask some friends, teachers, coaches, or family members what they think your strong qualities are. This can probably open your eyes to things you didn't think about yourself. We are our own worst critics and sometimes we put ourselves down so much we become oblivious to actually how awesome and talented we are. Again, it's natural to feel this way.

Don't beat yourself up about it, pick yourself up, brush it off and keep it moving while acknowledging it. Just be aware of your strengths and weaknesses.

Personal Inventory Activity

List 5 things you are good at then list 5 people you can rely on for trustworthy advice. List 5 strengths and 5 weaknesses. Bonus: write out how you can improve in those areas where you struggle.

Strengths	Weaknesses
_____	_____
_____	_____
_____	_____
_____	_____
_____	_____
_____	_____
_____	_____

Talents	Trustworthy Adults

Start By Changing What You Can Control

We are starting with ourselves at the starting point because we can control what we do. We can control changing our lives, we can control changing our habits and daily activities.

Show me a man who hunts and I'll show you a man who eats. Show me a woman who reads and I'll show you a woman who learns. Show me a student that doesn't go to class and I'll show you a failure. Simple enough, right? You are what you do daily. So, we have to practice mindfulness to have better daily awareness.

Starting might be harder for some than others, but one thing for sure is we all have to start somewhere in order to go somewhere. The student success mindset starts with you, and where you start is right within. Why? Because what you have is plenty. You are always in the right spot at the right time. You are and have more than enough as a human being and student. And don't believe anyone who tells you otherwise.

The bottom has built more champions than privilege ever could. No matter how far you are in the semester or in life, no matter your resources and no matter your race or ethnicity, no matter your financial or social status, student success is achievable for you. Yes you. The person reading this book. You are awesome, you are phenomenal, you are more than capable of achieving your goals, hopes and dreams as long as you start to believe in yourself.

Your belief is what will be the driving force to your success as a student and professional. So, what you believe about yourself will determine how far you go in life. If your belief is limited, then your success will be limited. If your belief is unlimited then your success will be unlimited. This means it will have no limits, no caps, and no ceilings.

Reflection Activity

After taking inventory of yourself what did you find out about yourself? Anything new? Anything different? Anything the same? Anything you like or don't like? How was that experience? Was it insightful? Do you think it will help you? Do you think it's not necessary? Why? Or why not? Write a quick summary of the self-inventory experience. How did you feel before, during, and after the process? List below.

_____

_____

_____

_____

_____

_____

_____

START BY CHANGING WHAT YOU CAN CONTROL

Student Success

When I was in school, I had no purpose for being there other than the fact that my mom made me go. Also, my friends were there and staying home or being out in the street was boring if my friends were not there. I was not motivated to get up and go to school every morning and sometimes I was forced out of bed and out of the house.

I was a problem for my mom and my family and, most importantly, I did myself a great disservice because, ultimately, I was hurting myself when I didn't attend school. I was hurting myself and my future. I was also hurting those around me because I was distracting them from learning while setting a bad example for my family, friends, and peers.

I was not focused on being successful and no one taught me how to be a successful student. I didn't know what success was, and I definitely didn't want success for myself at that time. I just wanted to pass with a C average, which set the bar super low. Looking back, that was not a successful time period in my life.

That time period helped me to actualize the reason I wrote this chapter. I don't want the same thing for you as I did for my younger self. I want you to be totally aware and locked into becoming a successful student. I don't want you wandering aimlessly in the hall not knowing what you want from this school year. I don't want another second to go by where you are just going with the flow or following the crowd. No direction, no guidance, no target ... you're just there. That's not cool, that's not what's up, that's not who you are destined to be.

So, let's get into it, what exactly is student success? Student success is identifying on a personal level the type of goals and things you want to achieve while being a student. Student success is in the eye of the beholder.

For some, student success is getting all A's because you want to get an academic scholarship. Maybe you want to be accepted into an ivy league college or just want to personally challenge yourself. Maybe you want to see how far you can push past your limits. For some, it's passing all classes with at least a B.

It could be graduating on time, or passing all your classes with no write ups or detentions. It could be anything you want. But here is the catch, it has to challenge you! Let your goals get you outside of your comfort zone. They have to push you and sometimes have to pull you.

Barely passing all your classes could be your ideal situation. I get it. But I want you to be honest. Is that a challenge? Is that a struggle? Is that easy to achieve or hard to achieve? Is that pushing you to your limits? Is barely passing making you get outside of your comfort zone? Is that pushing you to the edge of greatness or mediocrity?

Whatever you set out to do, make sure it challenges you to be the best you can be. There's no shame in barely passing all of your classes. I mean that was me in high school and a lot of successful others didn't have the grades to match my success at that time. Let's just say I wasn't voted most likely to succeed in my high school yearbook, either.

But I defied the odds and ended up on the right side of the statistics. I was on a path of being dead or in jail. But barely passing all my classes allowed me access to get my diploma and get into college. It opened doors for me to set examples for all those who came after me.

It also granted me the ability to get a 3.6 and 3.8 GPA my freshman year of college. All that came after barely passing all my classes, which I considered student success at that time. I realized my potential late into my high school years. You don't have to be great to start but you must start in order to be great.

Now I want to address the opposite end of the spectrum because it's just as important as the latter. Here's what not to base your student success on. A lot of people base their success on societal standards, peer pressure, and parental expectations.

This is another recipe for failure. I am warning you now to be very cautious when selecting what you view as student success. Remember, it's based on you and what works for you. It's not based on you and what works for your friends, or based on you and what works for your parents. Now family and friends can help you identify what they believe would be beneficial for you or what they think are good options, but at the end of the day you have the final say.

When I was in school I wanted to make my parents especially proud of me. I also didn't want to disrespect their authority. I incorporated my beliefs and my parents' beliefs into my idea of success because I wanted them to feel they were involved and had a say in my life because they are my parents.

They did give birth to me, they did raise me, they did take care of me when I was sick, and they warned me about many different situations. If I had followed their direction, I would've avoided a lot of mistakes, heartaches, mess ups, surprises, and failures.

So remember, student success has nothing to do with what society makes you believe. It has nothing to do with social media peer pressure and nothing to do with peer pressure. It has everything to do with your choices and what you want for your life. If it's getting all A's, go for it. If it's having an 86 overall GPA, go for it. If it's making a sports team and maintaining a B average and working a job, so be it.

Student Success Definition Activity

How do you define student success and why? Write your answer in the space provided.

_____

_____

_____

_____

_____

_____

_____

_____

_____

Why = Power = Fuel

What is your *why*? Your why is your fuel, it helps you stay focused and energized. I like to look at *why* as fuel because it fuels my weaknesses and makes them strengths. It gives me the energy I need to push past the pain. *Why power* is a game changer.

When I'm ready to give up and I'm ready to give in, I lock my thoughts on my why power. This helps me block out what's in front of me so I can have tunnel vision on my tasks and goals. Our brain tends to magnify everything we think about. We make the smallest things significant and the monumental things minor.

This is a natural process because it's your brain's way of preparing and/or protecting you from what lies ahead. It's a natural self-preservation process the brain puts you through because it always wants to protect you from harm. In order to combat this innate feature in your brain you have to develop your why. Developing your why is like anything else. It's a process, not a pill. Most of the time, people are looking for a quick fix or a magical one-time pill. What if it's not a pill, but a process? Would you still want it? There are no magical pills, foods, or drinks you can take to develop something overnight. Be leery of any salesman trying to sell you an overnight success product, 9 times out of 10, it's not legit.

Your why and motivation, are the same thing. It's just another way of asking, "What's your reasoning for doing what you do? Do you have enough reasons? Or do you have more excuses? Adults pay bills because they want the comfort of living in a house with heat, food, and electricity. So, adults are motivated to get a job in order to make the money that provides their wants and needs.

People also want relationships with friends, family, and significant others like boyfriends, girlfriends, husbands and wives. So, they use that as motivation, why power, or their reasoning for being honest, trustworthy, fun, outgoing, and good communicators. People will adopt any other characteristic that people will find cool or acceptable so others will want to spend time with them.

Who really wants to hang out with someone who lies, steals, deceives, hurts, manipulates or abuses others, or acts all types of negative? Not me. I choose my friends very wisely because you are who you hang with. I'll dive deeper into that in the next chapter. For now, let's focus on how to choose and develop your why power. Sound good? Let's go.

What is it that keeps you motivated, besides money? I say that because money is a given, it's easy and it's a necessity. We all need money to buy food, clothes, houses, etc. Your motivation has to be deeper than money because that is not a good enough reason to go through large amounts of pain and discomfort.

Think about it like this, if a dog stood between you and money, most people would not attempt to get the money because it's too risky. Your life is way too valuable. But, if a dog stood between you and your mom then you would feel more motivated to save your mom. Most people would risk their lives for someone they love. Who or what you love becomes your why power/motivation.

Someone or something paid for that thing you have. It may not be with money but they paid for it with their time, energy, blood, sweat and tears. We all have to give something every day in order to get something. Embrace this concept because you can't escape it. Running from it will benefit you nothing. But running *to* it and running *through* it will benefit you everything (read that 3x over).

So, who or what do you love enough that you're willing to risk it all for? What are you willing to sacrifice in order to succeed? What are you willing to give up in order to get up? Life is give and take. Something for nothing, doesn't exist. Literally!

Why Activity

What is your why? List 3 people who you would risk it all for.

_____

_____

_____

_____

_____

_____

_____

_____

_____

_____

WHY = POWER = FUEL

Circle of Influence

There will be a lot of jewels dropped in this chapter. You best believe that! This might be one of the most important sections in the book. Get your highlighter ready, underline, star it, whatever. Pay close attention to the principles and strategies in this chapter.

These four things help shape your circle of influence: environment, information, association, and experiences.

Your circle of influence are the people closest to you a.k.a. your friends, family, neighborhood, and social media followers. This is your circle of influence because these four groups influence you the most in life. One reason is because these people are the closest ones to you. They are close in proximity so they are easily accessible, comfortable, and convenient.

There is nothing wrong with comfort and convenience. However, there is a time to get uncomfortable and try new things, meet new people, experience different people, places and do different activities in life. Then your comfort zone becomes your biggest enemy because it creates complacency and keeps you from trying, stretching and challenging yourself. Stretch your comfort zone by adding new friends to your network, challenge your comfort zone by creating new and challenging goals like a 30-day push up challenge. Try new foods and go to new restaurants in different parts of town. Do new activities like clay molding, skateboarding, trying a new sport, or going for a hike in a new park.

1. Environment is where you live and where you spend most of your time. Environment for the most part determines what you do and think on a daily basis. I used to live in the hood. Trash everywhere, concrete buildings sky high, broken down houses, and the streets were littered with the drug addicts and gang members. This influenced the way I looked at life.

This made me feel like I belonged there. I felt one with the community. My family and friends shared the same environment. So, it made it that much easier to cope with. I was satisfied and happy with my situation. I accepted it until I got exposed to a different environment on a repeated basis.

So, the lesson here is get exposed to new environments, places, and people.

Window shop in the mall, view mansions on the Internet, go on vacation with family or friends, explore your city, and read books describing different countries, places, and people. Expose your mind to a new way of living and life on a repeated basis. Don't become a product of your environment by only accepting what's in front of you.

After a while, I didn't accept poverty, I didn't accept the hood and I didn't accept my current situation. I knew there was more for me. I knew there was more for my friends and family. Acceptance is doing nothing to change your situation. So, if you do nothing to change then, by default, you accept your environment.

2. Information is what you are gathering and/or learning from the people closest to you. We gather information by what we read, hear, see, feel, and experience. Are your friends interested in reading books or only playing video games? What about sports? Do you play sports more than you study?

What do you talk to your friends about on a daily basis? Is it about growth and leveling up? Or is it about complaining about school and parents? Is it about the latest trend on social media or is it about how you will be better students and people? Is it fashion-focused or boy/girl drama? What about gossiping and new hairstyles?

Don't get me wrong, it's okay to have regular discussions about fun stuff, cool stuff, and current events. But is that always the conversation? If so, start changing the conversation here and there. Start introducing new discussion topics. Discuss things that you rarely talk about and watch the magic happen.

Start reading self-help books and watching documentaries. Start researching and listening more often. God gave us two ears and one mouth because he wanted us to listen twice as much as we spoke. Listening is a skill. It's your ability to hear and not to respond, but listening to understand. Reading flexes the brain muscle like curls flex your arm muscle. The more you use it the more it grows.

Learn as much as possible; experience as much as possible. Do for the sake of doing. Learn for the sake of learning and experience for the sake of creating experiences. Become a scientist. Start experimenting. Start tracking. Start recording important dates in a journal. As a scientist, the objective is not to be right or wrong, or to pass or fail. The idea is to experiment.

Get as close to the truth as possible. Form hypothesis and ideas and test them. Scientist aren't worried about failure because it's a part of the process. It's a chance to learn. It brings new information and allows for you to experiment even further. And lastly, it brings you one step closer to success or the truth.

3. Association is who you hang with. Even if your intentions are pure, you are guilty by association. I remember when an officer at my high school told me I was a good kid and he was worried that I would end up dead or in jail not because of what I was doing, but because of who I was doing it with.

I used to hang with drug dealers and gang bangers, shooters, and smokers. I did none of these things at that time, but those people were literally family and friends. I was innocent, I wasn't in the streets, I was around the streets. I was like decoration on the block. You know how lights go on the Christmas tree for decorative purposes? I was the lights, not the tree.

I was the kid who, if they shot at my cousins and if I was to get hit, it would be a case of wrong place, wrong time. I was never the target. I was never the main focus. I was never that guy or big man on the block. But when the cops stretched us or pulled us over, I was guilty by association every time. People used to ask me why was I hanging there if I didn't participate?

I would always tell them because they are family. I learned this the hard way, but sometime you have to love family from a distance. Sometime you have to walk alone. It's tough and can get lonely, but it's absolutely necessary.

If you can't change who you hang with. Then change who you hang with. Read that again slowly. If you can't stop hanging with Tim, James, and John. Then change Tim, James, and John. How do you change them? Introduce new ideas to them. New games. New thoughts. Not in a controlling or negative way. But in a way that's beneficial to everyone. If you introduce new things to your friends or circle and they don't gravitate towards it, after you try once, twice or three times, then that's a good indication it might be time to change who you hang with and get new friends. For example, if they want to play football and you repeatedly introduce basketball to them but they don't want to play. Emphasis on repeatedly. Once could be a coincidence or mistake, but if you try multiple times and they still don't budge ...

It's time now to get new friends because you couldn't change the people who you were hanging with.

It's easier for the nine people to convince the one person to do what the majority are doing. It's ten times harder for the one person to change the other nine. Don't change the nine, stop trying, stop giving chances, just stay in your lane and attract others. There are a ton of people interested in what you do, find them. Don't sweat the others because the more confident you become within yourself, the more attractive you become to others. Confidence looks cool.

The longer you stay in that circle, the harder it will be for others to recognize you. I used to run with my hood. People thought I was gangsta even though I used to like to dance, sing, rap, watch anime, and go on adventures in nature. But all that was overshadowed by the fake image I put on as being gangsta and being around gangstas.

I wasn't being myself because I was faking and trying to fit in. I hid a lot of my true self so I could fit in with my circle. It was more beneficial to be like them and risk my life rather than be by myself. Of course, we had things in common. I liked sports, I liked to listen to rap music, and play outside. But that wasn't what I really wanted to do.

I was more popular, feared, and liked because I was with who I was with. I made a decision to fake it for the benefits and I sold myself out for the local popularity and notoriety. I got more attention that way.

It wasn't good attention, but nonetheless it was attention. It was for all the wrong reasons, but I was acknowledged. I was noticed and was offered assistance and help. I got more attention than the kids who were actually doing good.

It was an ego thing. I liked the attention and wanted more of it. I wasn't getting a lot of attention at home and by 16, I was basically on my own paying bills, grocery shopping, and staying out as late as I wanted. I had very little parental influence, so I had to grow up sooner rather than later.

Keep in mind, doctors hang with doctors, lawyers hang with lawyers, and athletes hang with athletes. Same goes for negative influences. Thieves hang with thieves, liars with liars and failures with failures. They get along because they have that one thing in common. I heard a theory once that was mind-numbingly accurate.

The theory goes: you are the sum total of the people you hang with. For example, take your top 5 friends, add their GPAs together to get a total, and then divide by 5. The answer you get would be your GPA or very close to it.

I dare you to try it with your closest friends and see the results. I did and I was blown away by how true it was. For example, in history class I had 3 really close friends. Let's say their names were Franky, Jaden, and Adenn. Franky's GPA was 77, Jaden's was 75, and Adenn's was 73. Add those 3 numbers up and get 225. Next divide 225 by 3 and you get 75. That 75 was also my grade point average. Now you try below. Choose your closest friends in any subject. Not the smartest people you know, but your real friends. Be honest. This is for your well-being. It was already proven true for me. I was the same grade level as the people I spent the most time with. (See the exercise at the end of this chapter)

4. Experience is what is happening to you. Better yet what is happening for you. What are you going through? What have you been through? What is affecting you? What is stopping you? What is fueling you? Who is inspiring you? Who is encouraging you? What are you experiencing that you like or dislike? Your experiences with people, places, and things shape your reality. And it rounds off your circle of influence.

If you have experienced some traumatic things in life, you're more likely to be shy, awkward, and timid around people. If you experience a lot of love, hugs, and encouragement you're more likely to give that which you receive. If you experience people cursing you out, yelling at you, and disrespecting you then you're more likely to exhibit those behaviors because they are learned behaviors.

So, when you are displaying actions you find weird or uncommon it's more likely you are exposed to it or have experienced it and now you are acting it out. Change the experiences by changing the people, environment, and actions. If you want more, do more. These are old clichés, but so true. If you want more love show more love. If you want better friends, be a better friend. If you want more happiness, make more people happy.

It all starts and ends with your experience. It all starts within you and works its way out of you. Hurt people, hurt people. Don't allow your experiences to permanently scar you. Remember we are not our first thought. Our first thought is our programing and conditioning. That's what we were made to believe over time, which necessarily isn't the truth, but is actually far from it.

It's what you think and do after your first thought that defines you. For example, if you see someone in the hall and have no knowledge of who they are, you may think negatively of them. This isn't right because you don't know or have any experience with them. Now if we get that thought and clean it up by saying, *I don't know this person they might be as nice as I am.* Then we train our brain to eliminate prejudice and find the good. You know what they say: Never a judge a book by its cover.

GPA Estimator Activity

You are the sum total of the people you hang with. For example, take your top 5 friends, add their GPAs together to get a total, and then divide by 5. The answer you get would be your GPA or very close to it.

_____

_____

_____

_____

_____

_____

_____

_____

_____

_____

CIRCLE OF INFLUENCE

Peer Pressure Awareness

I received a lot of unspoken peer pressure. What do I mean by unspoken peer pressure? The type of peer pressure that I didn't have to verbally hear for me to feel it. It is indirect and unspoken. Judging others is another form of peer pressure. Constantly and repeatedly asking and forcing someone to do something, or not do something, is another form of peer pressure. I'll give you examples.

All of my friends were failing in school and if you were passing, they treated you like an outcast. That's indirect peer pressure, knowing something isn't right and following the crowd in fear of standing out and being different. Feeling the judgmental vibe from looks and indirect and direct comments. It's when friends are acting funny by suddenly switching up how they act around you and others. Talking to you differently and acting differently are also signs

When a friend wants to cheat on a test and tries to bribe you with "I'll give you this or I'll tell everyone that" this is a form of peer pressure. Basically, whenever you feel pressured, forced, scared, ashamed, or you feel something heavy weighing you down in a negative way, this is bad peer pressure.

Dealing with peer pressure starts with acknowledging peer pressure exists and that it's affecting you. Pretending it doesn't exist and acting like you don't go through it will only make it harder on yourself. It will be harder for you to ask for help and it will be more difficult for others to help you. Understand this: peer pressure never goes away. Adults deal with pressure. There is no age limit to peer pressure.

Peer pressure can be people picking on you for the way you dress, act, think or feel. People will find any reason to try and put you down when they are insecure in their own skin. They are not well, are hurting inside and they want others to feel that same pain. This is why they act out in a bullying way.

If you have a peer, or someone who is in equal standing to you in age or profession; then you are susceptible to peer pressure. In the age of information and the Internet, peer pressure is heavily mixed in with social media. Having access to the internet has increased visibility to other people's lives, failures, and accomplishments.

If you have experienced low self-esteem, you can become influenced in a negative way by being jealous or envious of other people's accomplishments and advancements. When someone posts an achievement, like they made $100, someone will bring negativity and say that's nothing that's not even $1,000.

That's a negative response because how would the person making the comment know what the other person's end goal is? What if they only ever made $50 before? Making $100 is a great accomplishment because they just made double. They didn't even say, "congratulations" or "that's what's up." The first thing they did was move to challenging or downplaying the other person's success. No matter how big or small it is, it's a win to them.

This is something we have to be mindful of when being on social media. Be aware of backhanded compliments and other snarky negative "compliments". Social media is a breeding ground where haters, negativity, and bad attitudes flourish. Social media gives all the circus clowns and side acts a stage and an audience. Don't get caught up in the hype; everybody on social media is not winning. It's their highlight reel. It's about 5 to 10 percent of who they actually are.

Social media is an environment for the fakes, phonies, and liars to pretend to be something they are not. These people have always been around. This mindset and behavior have been here since the beginning of time. It's just now on display for the whole world to see with the advancement of technology and everyone having access to the World Wide Web.

Luckily, just like life, social media is a double-edged sword. Some people use it to speak life or use it to speak death. You can use it to do good or bad. You can use it for your benefit or your detriment. Just like life, it's up to you. You can choose to be successful or you can choose to be average.

How I dealt with peer pressure was by distancing myself and building my self-confidence. I got tired of people treating me like an outcast for not agreeing with them. I got tired of going against my better judgement. I know I was right, based on the facts and context and refused to go with the crowd because it was the popular opinion at the time. I accepted I was different. I accepted that others were different. That's the difference. No one is better than someone else, just different. Here are three ways to boost your self-confidence:

1. Define cool. Don't allow others to say what's cool and what's not. You move by the beat of your own drum. You make the decision and allow others to make theirs. Let them do their thing while you do yours.

2. Affirm it. Say what you mean and mean what you say. Every day, say a positive affirmation. The brain is a creature of habit and repetition. The more you say it, the more you will believe it. Repetition is mastery.

3. Practice. Again, train your brain. Train your body. Do the work. Even when you don't feel like it. Practicing public speaking will make you more confident. So, whatever you feel weak in, practice it. Remember practice makes progress and progress makes perfect. The better you are at doing something, the more self-confident you will be.

Positive peer pressure is when a friend challenges you to get better grades. That's a form of good peer pressure. Or, when a friend tries to get you outside of your comfort zone to stay away from bad company. That's pressure pushing you to make good decisions. Positive influences and people assisting in helping you achieve your goals, are all signs of good peer pressure. Allow that pressure to take you to the next level. Allow it to mold you, shape you, and make you the best you can be.

Managing Expectations

Managing expectations will bring peace of mind and understanding in any relationship with parents, friends, and school staff. Here's how to manage expectations. Start by defining words and phrases, so both parties are on the same page. Come to a common ground to bring about a common understanding. This way, no one is expecting any more or less than what both parties agreed upon. This helps each person hold the other accountable.

Some people live with parents that apply a lot of pressure to get good grades. Some families have very high standards, especially if you come from a successful family. Some families have no expectations at all and are proud of everything or sometimes nothing. This can be a good or bad thing. It's all about how you handle pressure and manage expectations. Some people rise to the occasion and some people fold under pressure.Pressure either bursts pipes or makes diamonds. Allow pressure to make you into a diamond.

I will give you the strategies to help you deal with the pressure from family and how to help manage their expectations of you. I know it can be tough and seem unfair when trying to manage the expectations from parents. But we all have to go through it and I am here to tell you that you can and will get through it.

Here are some tips for dealing with overbearing parents with extremely high standards. Have an open line of communication with your parents and or legal guardians. Don't hide what you believe or feel, express it in a well-mannered and respectable format. Tell them your point-of-view and give them reasons why you believe what you do. Most parents are open to accept what you are saying if you are able to back it up with sound logic and reasoning.

Don't be dismissive, insensitive, and condescending. Be lighthearted, open-minded and willing to listen to their point-of-view and if you cannot reach a conclusion, try postponing the conversation for a later date where you revisit the topic.

If that doesn't work, try compromising. A compromise is where both parties have a mutual agreement to both have a say in the conclusion. Both parties have an end gain in the agreement and a say in how each will go about achieving this agreed upon expectation.

For example, let's say you want to get a C in math because math isn't your strongest topic. But your dad wants you to be an engineer and get an A in math. So, you compromise and say I'll try for a B if you pay for a tutor. I'll make it to all the sessions and also get weekly or monthly progress reports. Now both parties have mutual arrangements in the agreed upon end result.

Lastly, try adding a trusted unbiased third party to help alleviate the situation and be the voice of reason for both parties. Consider asking a grandparent or other trusted adult. Some people use church pastors or counselors and maybe even a coach. If all else fails, follow the directions of your parents. They created you and raised you so they know a thing or two about life.

Also, you will not be under their rule your entire life. At some point, they will let go of the reigns and allow you to make every decision for your own life. Once you're not under their roof or on their payroll, then you will have the freedom and leverage to make all the decisions and without parent interference. As of now, take a big slice of humble pie and enjoy it. Some people go through life wishing they had parents who care as much as yours do. They have a lot of life experience to give, so never shut your ears and eyes to their wisdom, they do it all out of love.

Remember, knowledge is a tool. You can use it or not, if you so choose. For example, if you want to build a house, a basic tool you would need is a hammer. But if you never go and get the hammer, you will not be able to build the house. So, get the information (tool) and build yourself a house (school expectations), and live by it.

No, for real, live by it. Don't go a day without seeing it. Don't go a day without thinking about it. Why? Because out of sight, out of mind. What you think about and focus on, you attract. Your thoughts are like magnets. The more you think about it, the more likely you will see and get it.

If it's not in front of your eyeballs, sometimes you will forget what you set out to do. Writing things down is like magic. Here is a cool example someone shared with me. Witches, wizards, warlocks, and magicians cast spells, right? We usually see casting spells or spelling in a supernatural way in movies and cartoons. They make magic potions, or use a magic wand to throw fire balls etc. In reality, when spelling or casting spells we use words, and our magic wand is our pen or pencil. So, when you write on paper you are casting spells like magic. What's the magic? Making your dreams come true. Watching your thoughts and ideas go from paper to the reality. The airplane started in someone's mind then went onto paper. They drew it out. They spelled it, drawing in a sense, is spelling but in picture form. Next thing you know, humans were in the sky with the birds. Now that's like magic, or at least super close to it. That's amazing if you ask me. That's the real wow factor, right there. That's why writing is like casting spells because when you write it down you can bring it to life, just like magic. Making something out of nothing. Turning your thoughts into things.

I'll give you another example. I wrote a list of goals. One was to make the dean's list in college. I did this before the semester started and at the end of the semester, poof like magic, there I was written on the school website amongst all the other students who made the dean's list. With hard work and dedication, I accomplished the goal I wrote on paper.

You probably have a ton going on in your life from personal, social, and academic levels. You are only human; you can't remember everything. If you look at it three times a day, once in the morning, once in the afternoon, and once at night, it will become embedded in your memory. Over time, you will no longer need to read from the paper.

Remember this: people forget, paper doesn't!

Expectation Activity

Now I want you to list the expectations you have for yourself. What do you want to accomplish or achieve this marking period, semester, or school year? What do you expect of friends and family? What are some challenges you might face while trying to achieve this goal? Talk this over with your friends, parents, and trusted professional adults so as to get a well-rounded view of all of your expectations.

_____

_____

_____

_____

_____

_____

_____

Balance and Rhythm

Balance is the ability to move or remain in a position without losing control or falling. Rhythm is a regularly repeated pattern of movement or actions. Both are super important when trying to have a better experience in school. They both go hand-in-hand when trying to maintain a certain amount of changes that are bound to happen anyway.

If you would have asked me in high school to explain what balance and rhythm meant I would have not been able to tell you. I could have given you an example - maybe. I could have given an idea of the two words, but I literally never had balance or rhythm until I was in the last years of my college experience. I believe this was way too late.

I believe the sooner we start to be aware of our daily routine and habits the better position we will be in to achieve our goals.

There is power in consistency, a.k.a. routine. Why? Because little-by-little, a little becomes a lot. Let's look at it in terms of money. Say, every time you get a dollar you spend a dollar. A dollar is a little bit of money until 100 days go by and you end up spending all $100. Every time you got it; you gave it away. Or, if you get a paycheck and save 10 percent of it.

Over time, with consistency, that 10 percent over 10 weeks will be a whole paycheck. It added up little by little. This is what you call the slow and sustainable method. It's not flashy, it's not fast, it's not glamorous, and it's not interesting, but it works.

One thing I noticed is people get caught up in the get rich quick scheme. They get attracted to it because it's flashy, it's fast, it doesn't take long, and it's like an adrenaline rush. Don't be that person caught up in the hype. It's not worth it. Learn from the mistakes of those who came before you and consider your ways. Choose something that's sustainable and not built on a shaky foundation.

Learning to schedule your day will help you get in a rhythm. You will know when you are off balance when you start to break away from your routine. It will mess up your rhythm and slow down your momentum. Another word for scheduling is time management. I want you to focus on making a schedule of your day-to-day activities and obligations.

What time do you wake up? What time are you at school? What time are you with friends and family? Are you involved in any social clubs? If so, from what time of the day? This will help you have a better understanding of your 24 hours. If you want to be a successful student then making an outline of your day will help you get three steps ahead of the game. Take a quick survey and ask your friends who have a daily outline of their 24 hours?

Most likely, the answer will be less than 10 percent and if you fit in that category, how are you going to stand out when it's time to be considered for a college or job application? The answer is you won't, unless you do something different.

This is an awesome opportunity because you have the potential to do a lot of things different and scheduling your day is a great place to start to make separation between you and the rest of the world.

We cannot stop, start, fast forward, rewind, or pause time. It's just not possible! Time continues to tick day in and day out, even as we try to figure it out. Everybody has time, but most do not use it to their advantage.

When I was in school, I was a serious procrastinator. I mean, if I had a week before the assignment was due, I started and finished the night before, in most cases. Scheduling study time was not even in my vocabulary. Time management was also a skill I had no desire to develop in school, I saw no use for it. I was just going with the flow. I would skip class if everyone else did it and I wouldn't do my homework because homework was for lames and soft dudes. We didn't go around the halls congratulating each other about the good things in school, we made jokes instead. Lastly, what I want you to know is no one starts out perfect. No one gets it right at the same time, all the time. So, don't put too much pressure on yourself.

Time Management Activity

In the space below, develop your ideal day from wake up to bedtime. Schedule your ideal day. Yes, that means scheduling your sleep time. For example, what are you doing between the following time frames each day:

6 a.m. to 8 a.m.

8 a.m. to 10 a.m.

10 a.m. to 12 p.m.

12 p.m. to 2 p.m.

2 p.m. to 4 p.m.

4 p.m. to 6 p.m.

6 p.m. to 8 p.m.

8 p.m. to 10 p.m.

10 p.m. to 6 a.m. Let's say this is your sleep time. Eight hours a day.

BALANCE AND RHYTHM

Goal Setting

Goal setting is super important when talking about student success. After all, how can you be successful without accomplishing anything? When I was in high school and college, I never set the expectations high. I never raised my standards and I did not believe in myself until the tail end of my high school career.

I never wrote my goals on paper and I only made goals during the semester *after* I saw some progress in the class, which made me adjust accordingly. I never went into the semester with the expectation that I would get all A's or all B's because I did not believe in myself. I was not confident in my ability to learn or my capacity to retain information.

If I was getting C's to begin the semester, I would just shoot for a C. I based my goals on things I could see when I should have based my goals on things I couldn't see. If I would have set goals differently earlier, I would have forced myself to work harder, study longer, get a tutor, and or create study groups with my peers.

Why should you write down your goals? Because words cast spells and spelling is magic. That's right, what you write down comes to life. What you think about and visualize most always appear in your reality. If you think negative thoughts all day and see negative things in your daily life, 9 times out of 10, you will experience some negative things that day. The same goes for positive thinking and seeing positive actions. You will ultimately experience something positive in your life because you were surrounded by good, positive thoughts.

Writing goals the S.M.A.R.T. way is the first step in goal setting. S.M.A.R.T. is an acronym for Specific, Measurable, Action, Relevant, and Timeline. This is one of many methods you can use to start creating a detailed plan for achieving your goals this school year. You can also use this formula for the rest of your life. I used this formula in college and still use it till' this day.

S.M.A.R.T. goals are a classic and timeless method to organize a detailed plan for your goals, so it will never go out of style because it's just too rich in practicality. Let's walk through an example of how to use this newfound information. First, we have to break it down so you understand why and how to do it.

I don't want you regurgitating information. I want you very educated about the process so you can teach it to others, as well, and allow it to create a lasting impression in your memory.

The **S** is for **Specific**, we must be very specific in our goal. You don't want to leave any room for misunderstanding and confusion. Make your goals as specific and to the point as possible, so it's clear as day in your mind and on paper. Specificity will leave no room for guesswork, confusion, or maybes. We will be definite and intentional about what we want to do and how we want to accomplish it.

For example, if you are a C grade level student, your specific goal can be going from a C to a B. is that specific enough? What if we said my overall grade in science is a 72 and by the end of the marking period I want my overall grade to be an 80, or above. Which example do you believe is more specific?

The **M** is for **Measurable**, how will we measure this goal? What standard will we use to determine if we are making progress, staying stagnant, or regressing? Measuring makes it real. If you cannot measure it, how will you know if you are making progress or not? Is progress a feeling? Is it intangible or is it tangible? Can we see it, hear it, taste it, touch it, smell it, or weigh it? Or is it the opposite, and we can't use our five senses to keep track of it? Think about it like this, if you want to go from a 72 to an 80 how would you measure that? What you should do first is find out what contributes to your grade point average. Usually it consists of tests, attendance, quizzes, and participation.

So, you can measure it by keeping track of how you are doing in those specific categories. Keep an eye on them daily, weekly or monthly. If your test grades are a C every time, keep track of it in a journal or wherever you keep your notes. Have a teacher give you or your parents a progress report, so you can keep track of attendance and participation.

There is nothing worse than thinking you're making progress, just to find out that you are not on the same page as your teacher. Imagine how it feels to think that you're participating and working hard and you think you're doing awesome. You're excited to see your new grade and you have been bragging about it to your parents and friends. On the day report cards come out; you didn't raise your GPA at all. That would suck tremendously, right? It wouldn't feel good, but all that could have been avoided if you would have just kept track and or measured how you were doing throughout the semester. Then you would not have to worry about your grades, you would already know.

Let's say you and your teacher have two different grades at the end of the marking period. At least now you would have a legitimate argument and proof that your grade was incorrect and the evidence to support why it should be corrected. Staying on top of your grades and having the awareness to check them is a great identifier that you want to make serious change towards becoming a successful student and getting better grades.

Winners are trackers. Track your progress, like athletes track weight, speed, and strength. Business's track inventory, expenses, and income. School tracks, grades, participation, and attendance. Tracking helps with self-awareness.

The **A** is for **Action**. What steps will you take to insure you follow through on your goals? This will require certain specific actions that you can perform during the S.M.A.R.T. process. What action steps do you have in mind that you can make immediately?

These do not need to be major steps, by the way. Major change is not usually a result of one major action. Major change is usually the results of lots of little actions taken consistently over time. Over time, these steps add up and/or compound into major results. Overthinking and bombarding yourself with too many tasks to handle at one time is what will throw you off track.

These are action *steps*, which is plural. Not action *step*, meaning you will do one thing, one time and your grades will change as a result of it. Although this *could* happen, but it is highly unlikely. The probability is very low and it's too high risk to take a chance on, so don't waste time waiting for a miracle.

You can put a plan together that requires you to take repeated actions. Then go back over the plan to see if it's working and if the steps you are taking are having a positive impact. keep them going and remove the steps that are not working so much and add new ones, if necessary.

Sometimes you just might have to remove some steps and don't add anything. Sometimes you will need to add some things onto the things you are already doing. There will also be times that you need to add *and* take away. Whatever is required of you, be willing to do it in order to achieve your goal. Some of the steps you might have to take might include setting apart more time to study. I am talking about devoting hours a day to mastering a subject or preparing for a test.

Moving forward, the letter **R** is for **Relevant**. How is this goal relevant to you in your life? Is this goal realistic or is it far-fetched? You want to make sure your goals are relevant to what's important to you. It isn't relevant based on what society says your goals should be, or what society views as relevant.

Your goals are not what your parents think is relevant nor what your closest friends say is relevant. This is about what's relevant to you and your dreams. Your vision, your aspirations, your accomplishments, and your feelings are the focus here. This isn't selfish, even though in some areas of your life, sometimes you have to be selfish. This isn't one of them.

Continuing on with the example of getting better grades, how is that relevant to you? Will getting better grades help you be more educated? Of course, they will. Will getting better grades help you get into college? 100 % facts. Will getting better grades help inspire other people like your family and friends? Yes, because if they see you can do it, that will inspire them and help them to feel like they can achieve that, too.

I'll never forget the day my wife graduated from Syracuse University. My 11-year-old nephew was there and he saw the inside of the football stadium. It was larger than life to him.

As we were leaving after the graduation I asked if he wanted to go to Syracuse University one day, or at least go to college. He said "yes for sure!" Seeing his aunt graduate from a major university inspired him to believe he also would be able to graduate from a major college, as well.

Seeing is believing, and being exposed to Syracuse University made graduating college ten times more real to him.

So, getting better grades is very relevant to a student in many different ways. It will not only benefit you, but will also benefit others. When goal setting, figure out how it is relevant to you and your future.

Let's discuss what is not relevant to your grades when goal setting. You need to know what not to do as well as what to do. Partaking in these activities will actually slow you down in the process. will not help you get better grades, become a better person, nor will it help you set a good example for your family, friends, and those in your community.

I remember when I was in college and I was on Facebook. I was partying, skipping class, not studying, hanging in the café, watching too much TV, and posting inappropriate things because I thought I was cool. But in reality, I was making myself look bad to potential employers and my younger nieces and nephews. These things did not help me to accomplish anything and they were not relevant to my future. They were not relevant to my career neither were they helping me grow as a person.

I was doing it just to fit in. I was doing it to be a part of the crowd, when I had no business being in *that* crowd. I was continuing in a cycle that did not lead to success, financially, mentally, physically, and/or emotionally. It was safe to say that if I stayed on that route, nothing good was coming my way.

Last but not least, the **T** stands for **Timeline**. These goals must be timed because you don't have 10 years to complete a goal that, on average, with little effort most people can get done in four years. In life, most everything has a timeline or a due date, but especially in the world of academia, a.k.a. school.

From K-12, college, and graduate school all assignments have due dates. Even when you are in the house, if your mom gives you an assignment, it has a time in which it needs to be done. When you get a driver's license, you have a certain amount of time before it has to be renewed. If it's not renewed within the time allowed it will be expired.

Most things surrounding your life have a timeline or a due date. Adding a due date helps you to stay aware and keep track of how much time you spend on a subject or know when an assignment is due. This adds an extra layer of pressure to the situation. Pressure is seen as negative to most people.

I am going to share a secret with you today that you can carry with you for the rest of your life. Pressure is positive. Most people feel pressure and don't know how to deal with it so it impacts them negatively. But when you understand pressure and develop a positive relationship with pressure situations you become more experienced and know how to handle pressure.

When I was younger, I didn't know how to handle pressure and I didn't like to read aloud. I didn't like to come out of my comfort zone because I was afraid I would embarrass myself. I didn't try my hardest because I didn't want to seem wrong or be wrong.

I cared way too much about what people thought of me. I allowed their judgements to determine how I lived my life. I allowed societal pressures to keep me from becoming my best self. But after realizing pressure is positive, I unleashed my inner potential. I allowed pressure to push me to be greater. I allowed pressure to propel me to success, and I used pressure as a tool for motivation. The more pressure the better because I knew that pressure was a way my body prepared me for the task ahead. When I felt the nervousness in my stomach, I knew that was my body's way of telling my brain that I was amped up and ready to go.

When I was younger, I thought that feeling was nervousness holding me back and telling me to be afraid. I thought it was telling me to run and quit because I wasn't ready. But that was my ignorance; that was the trick. The media tricked me into believing that the feeling was bad, but that feeling is actually so good. Without it you wouldn't know when you are ready to go. Nervousness and excitement are the same feeling. We choose what to call it. So when my hands get shaky and my stomach bubbles and knots up, that's when I'm triggered to say I'm so excited and ready for the challenge.

Most people associate nervousness with fear. But, what they are really doing is mixing nervousness with frozenness. You freeze because you don't know what to do. Heat makes you move. When you are warmed up, you are ready to go. When you freeze, you can't move.

It's like when you're exercising coaches recommend that you warm up first, right? They tell you don't stretch cold muscles because you aren't warmed up yet. When a basketball player makes a couple shots in a row, they say he is on "fire." Emphasis on fire because he has a rhythm, he is hot. When he misses multiple shots, they say he is cold because he isn't making anything.

This is a key concept, pay attention to the difference between nervousness and frozenness. A healthy amount of fear is required for success and accomplishment but freezing up or procrastinating is counterproductive. These are an enemy of success and everything you are trying to accomplish. It's ok to freeze in the beginning. Over time, as you learn to master your craft and control yourself, you will be able to overcome your feelings of being frozen. Freezing comes as a default defense mechanism when you're put in high pressure situations you are not comfortable with. As you warm up to these situations, you will be able to perform better under heavy pressure. The better you become, the easier it gets. So, don't ask that the situation be easier. But ask of yourself to be better, to be more knowledgeable, and to be more skillful and more in control.

Keep this in mind as you get closer to your finish line and/or due date. That's when it's crunch time. That's when the pressure is at its highest and you're coming to completion. Having a due date for assignments helps you keep track of your assignment status. You should know how much you need and when you need it by.

Remember done is better than perfect. If it's perfect most likely it will never be done.

This also keeps you, your parents, and teachers all on the same page when it comes to your progress. Knowing your status also gives you peace of mind while on your journey. When you don't know your status, you tend to be more anxious and not at ease because you lack the necessary information to calm yourself down.

Knowing where you stand clears your mind. Not knowing or being confused about where you stand leads to clouded judgement and a lot of unanswered questions, anxiety, frustration, and a lack of patience. You become restless and impatient when you don't know something.

Knowing allows you to rest assured and be patient because your questions have been answered. Pressure is going to get you going. Pressure is going to move you in the right direction. Pressure is going to make you go twice as hard. It gives you that extra boost of energy to help carry you across the finish line.

That pressure needs direction and the goal you are trying to accomplish is the director. Pressure without direction will make you freeze. If it doesn't, that's even worse because it's going to take you in a direction contrary to the finish line.

When it starts to take you in the wrong direction, it doesn't slow down. It only goes harder and speeds up. Pressure moves you. It's up to you to allow pressure to move you in the right direction. Don't choose to allow pressure to move you in the wrong direction.

I'll give you an example. I remember I had a major test coming up and I was not studying for it. I knew it was coming, but it wasn't a priority to me. It wasn't important to me and it wasn't an emergency, so I did what I wanted to do. I stayed up late, I went to the gym, played video games, went to friends' houses, watched TV, and scrolled through social media. As time went on, the date kept getting closer and closer. As pressure mounted, I used that pressure to keep me from studying.

I didn't know what I was doing at the time. I wasn't equipped with the information I have now. I was not aware of the mindset or the strategy needed to help me get out the situation. Instead, I just allowed myself to procrastinate. I was drifting further and further away from my studies.

I told myself, *why study? I'm going to fail anyway. Why bother? I can make it up with extra credit. I understand the topic … I will just take the test based on my memory, alone. I have done it so many times in the past, why not now? It has worked before … it will work again.* Mind you, in the past I was not an A student. I was not even a B or C student. But I always had false hope in myself, that when I do take the test I'll remember enough to pass.

Let's just say I did not pass that test. I was not a good test taker. Test taking was my weakest attribute in high school because I never studied. It's not a hard correlation to make. It's actually quite simple. Those who study, do better on tests and those who do not study do poorly when it comes to taking the test.

In conclusion, goal setting the S.M.A.R.T. way means:

Specific: What do you want to accomplish? Describe it in much detail.

Measurable: How will you keep track of your progress?

Action: What steps will you take to achieve this goal? What will you do and what will you avoid doing?

Relevant: How is this important to your life? Will it have immediate impact now, or future impact tomorrow?

Timeline: Put a due date on it and don't wait until the last minute to start. Give yourself a good amount of time based on the goal you are trying to achieve. The bigger the goal the longer the process. The smaller the goal the quicker the process.

S.M.A.R.T. Goal Activity

Identify and describe your S.M.A.R.T. goal in the space below.

_____

_____

_____

_____

_____

_____

_____

_____

GOAL SETTING

Study Habits

As a student, one of the most important things you can do is study. Studying is a habit, which in turn, will develop a skill. You are what you do on a daily basis. You create your habits and then your habits create you. Here is the thing, you do not become who you are by doing something once. If that was the case, it would be way too easy for people to accomplish their goals.

Imagine a world where all you would have to read was one book and boom you're a doctor. Imagine a world where all you would have to do was dribble a basketball and now you are one of the best basketball players to ever live. That's crazy to think about right? Mind blowing to me because that would be way too easy. Keep this in mind, if everyone can do it, no one can do it.

What do I mean? It becomes less impressive if everyone can do it. It becomes average and normal. There is no wow factor to it, right or right? So naturally when you see someone just running, you don't gather around the television for that. However, if it's the Olympics, you want to watch because those are the best runners in the world.

You want to see people who do the best magic tricks, people who play the best basketball, people who are the best doctors, that's who you want to take care of you. Those are the people who developed a habit and their habit turned into a skill and their skill turned them into one of the best.

Studying is literally a skill that has to be developed and it's different for everyone, so it's important to find out what works for you.

Study Strategy #1: Start a Peer-to-Peer Study Group

Studying with your peers is a great way to learn. This can be done with your friends and without. Be circumspect when studying with friends. Studying with friends can be very beneficial or detrimental. Most times, friends are distracting when it's time to lock in and focus.

Friends mean well and they may have your best interest at heart, but if the work is not getting done, then it's hurting more than helping. Sometimes friends don't understand the severity of the situation, which is ok. They don't have to take life, or even this situation, as seriously as you do.

But it's up to you to set the record straight with friends so you will able to achieve your goals. They may not understand in the beginning, but if they are your true friends they will give you your space and be happy when you come back to them ready to hang out. This is a sign of emotional maturity. To be able to let someone you love go and understand they will come back and it will be as if they never left.

Peer-to-peer study groups have their pros and cons. Let's go over a few shall we?

Pro #1

Openly sharing information. When you get to share what you know, you get to teach. And when you teach others, you get to learn a subject twice. This helps retain information and stick in your brain longer. You are more likely to be able to pull it out when the test comes. This also allows for higher retention levels.

Pro #2

You get to learn new information and hear it from a different perspective. Hearing how someone else breaks things down may be the inch you need to understand the subject better. That little bit of information, said in another way, may bridge the gap between what you didn't know and what you thought you knew.

Pro # 3

You can share notes from class. Some people take better notes than others and you may benefit from something someone else wrote, that you missed, and vice versa.

It's like using each other to fill in the blanks. If a puzzle has three pieces and each group member gets one piece, if you put your pieces together, then everyone has access to one puzzle. You might not have three different puzzles, but one is more than enough for the three of you. It's like forming Voltron. Or a Megazord. You are great individually, but way more powerful together.

Let's get into the cons of peer to peer study groups.

Con #1

The weaknesses of a peer-to-peer study group is sometimes no one in the group really understands the subject matter. If no one has a grip on the topic, then none of you can teach each other or share information.

Con #2

This a piggy back off of Con #1 and that is, when only one person has good notes and the others don't. It will be as if one person is doing all the teaching and everybody else is doing the learning. Basically, that one person is doing all the work and helping everybody, but is not getting help in return. They are left filling everyone else's cups, but no one is pouring into theirs.

It can make the person with the information feel like they are being taken advantage of because everyone else is not pulling their own weight.

Con #3

Some people may not be trustworthy to start a peer-to-peer group with. Make sure all the people in the group are responsible so you're not babysitting and wasting your time. They have to be reliable and dependable group members.

Study Strategy #2: Increase Your Reading Skill

Another form of studying, which is a basic yet absolutely vital tool is reading the material. You cannot overlook the fundamentals. The fundamentals are easy to overlook because they are not shiny, cool, or popular. The fundamentals are boring, tedious, and take time to develop.

Reading is a skill and some people have never developed this skill throughout their lifetime. Some people are in high school reading at a middle school grade level. This is not because they are incapable of reading, but they just don't want to take the time to develop the fundamentals. Put it like this: in basketball everyone wants to cross people over, but they can't even dribble with both hands. That's a fundamental aspect of the crossover. They are skipping steps because they see the crossovers of their favorite basketball player on television and want to emulate what that person is doing. But what they fail to realize is that it took time for that player to learn the fundamentals before mastering the cross over.

Spectators didn't see the time they put in during practice, the off season, and all the time they spent practicing dribbling drills and developing the habits that helped them get to the NBA or NCAA where they can showcase their skill and hard work.

Everybody wants the glory but overlook the story.

People like to judge how others are successful, but don't like to go through what they went through in order to become successful. People want the accolades, the money, the accomplishments, and the fame. However, they don't want the pain, the suffering, the sacrifice and the long days and nights it takes to achieve what they have.

So, in order for us to become better readers, which in turn will help make us better at studying, we must develop the habit of reading. Not just reading for the sake to say words on a piece of paper, but we must learn to read critically and analyze what we read.

One of the most surprising things I realized in school was the emphasis on putting things in my own words. This concept was introduced in middle school, but played a major factor in college.

I remember being in class in high school and the regents exams were coming up. It was the biggest exam at the end of the school year and you had to pass in order to graduate. It was a test that had multiple choice and a written exam. The multiple choice was the hardest part for me.

I didn't study at all in high school and I never read books outside of school hours. Luckily, I did enough in school to pass the exams. I thought I was ahead of the game, but in reality, I was not. I was way behind because I took that habit of not studying with me into college. I could have been ahead of the game or at least on a level playing field if I did what I was supposed to do when I was supposed to do it.

What I learned in college was that a good portion of the exam is based on the readings assigned in class. The test would consist of material we learned from lectures and material we were supposed to read on our own. Sometimes the test questions were verbatim from the book itself.

Do you see why reading is such an integral part of studying? If I would have just read and did the practice questions at the end of the chapter, I most likely would have went from a C student to, at minimum, a B student. Reading not only prepares you for the class discussions, but it also aids you in knowing what may be on the test and gives you a well-rounded understanding of the material.

Reading helps strengthen your brain like lifting weights help strengthen your body. Reading helps strengthen your brain and communication skills. How? By reading you can learn the meaning of new words and see how they are used in different contexts. Your vocabulary grows and, in return, you are able to learn to use those words in their proper context during conversation. Reading is one of the most important factors in getting a good education. If you are not able to read, then it will be harder, lots harder to get a well-rounded education.

Don't take reading for granted. I know reading is not the coolest thing, or the most fun, but cool things only go so far. Smart people go way further in life then cool people do. Having the information is more important than not having the information. Applied information is the difference between the haves and the have nots.

Reading is what will separate the A students from the C students. Reading is the gap that most people don't know exists because reading is not promoted in society as much as it should be. What if we stopped watching TV every day for 2 hours a day and instead encouraged people to read and study? Then people would be less distracted and more focused. People would be more accomplished and the world would be a much better place, in my opinion.

That's all it takes, some time and a minor shift in your daily habits. To begin, dedicate one hour a day to homework, study, and reading at a minimum. Challenge yourself to do something different so you will receive something different.

Nothing changes unless you change.

Study Strategy #3: Self-Quizzing

When studying for an important test. This is one of the best study strategies out there. I used this technique all the time. When learning new concepts create flashcards and for the questions that are easy, put them in one pile. For the ones a little more difficult, put them in another pile. Lastly, for the ones you get wrong, put them in a separate pile as well. Study the ones you got wrong first, second the difficult ones, and last the easy ones. When studying be sure to study in a peaceful area that is free from distractions. This helps prime you for an effective study session. Creating different work spaces allows the body to get ready for a certain activity. When you go to the gym you know you're getting ready for a high intense physical activity. Same with when you lie on your bed, your body knows it's time to sleep. Entering the kitchen signals that it's time to eat. So, when studying, if you pick a study spot - remain consistent with it. Your body will soon learn that it's time to study.

Studying is like working out in some ways. You don't need 8 hours in the gym every day. You just need high intensity workouts over a short period of time, consistently. Studying in small intense windows helped me with retaining the information a lot better and helped me to not overwhelm myself. I would study for no longer then 2-hour increments for no less then 45 minutes. This way, I was able to be strategic and save time for other activities. Trying to cram and study for 4 to 8 hours, last minute, really was ineffective for me. But small windows over time, while being patient with myself and telling myself, *you did a good job! Be proud.* That really helped boost my grades and confidence.

Positive self-talk is key in this part because if you tell yourself you didn't do enough or you did a bad job or you will never pass, it will really kill your motivation and drive to do better. Here is a strategy you can use when the negative thoughts try to kick in. for every negative thought, counteract it by saying something positive three additional times. That way, what you say more often will stick and the negative will fall off.

Lastly, when you are learning something new and you want it to stick, try relating it to something you already know and experienced. Make it so plain and so simple that if you were to explain it to a 5-year-old, they would understand what you are trying to say. This way, when the test comes and you run the information back in your head, it is simple. Try using study days to help retain info and not overwhelm yourself. Monday's are for Math, Tuesday's for History, Wednesday's for Science, Thursday's for Social Studies, etc., this way, you're not studying everything, every day and overwhelming yourself.

Don't wait for a teacher to assign you something to read. Read independently. Prioritize your reading materials. Start with the class material or assigned homework, if any. If there is nothing assigned for you to do, pick up a book and read it.

Read a book about whatever interest you. This is something easy to start with. Pick a book about your favorite television show or sport. Pick a book from your favorite celebrity or athlete. Get started by reading whatever you can get your hands on. This is a good practice for beginning your reading habit. Read whatever you can get from the public library or the school library. Start slow. Read for about 15 minutes a day to start. Try this for about 21 days. I was listening to Jim Kwik on his Kwik Brain Podcast on Spotify one day and he was talking about how an action repeated for 21 days is enough to start a new habit and or break old ones. Give it 21-30 days of consistent discipline and effort. I found this to be true when I put it to the test. I had a bad habit of eating sweets so I went on a 30-day fruit fast. No sweets at all. It was a challenge, but I overcame it. I also wanted to read more so, I challenged myself to read a page a day for 30 days straight. Now I love reading and have a goal to read 12 books in a calendar year.

After the time is up, go back and look at the results. See where you went right and see where you went wrong. Self-assess and make the necessary adjustments. Maybe reading directly after school didn't help and maybe it interfered with your homework schedule. Try reading before bed or in the morning. Maybe try reading after homework is done.

Successful people make adjustments and unsuccessful people make excuses. Which one do you want to be?

Bring It Home

In conclusion, I want to leave you with a couple quotes. "Life doesn't give you what you need unless you bring life a seed," Jim Rohn. I was listening to a YouTube video from Jim Rohn about goals and determination. In the video, he tells a story about a farmer who is on a farm and asks the earth to bear fruit.

He asks for what he needs from the earth, but the earth tells him, "Don't bring me your need, bring me your seed." I found this to be otherworldly inspiring. This message spoke to my soul and made me look at life totally different. It made me think outside the box. It enlightened me and what I learned from the message was this:

Don't go around complaining about what you need and what you don't have. Don't go around asking for handouts or shortcuts. Bring life your seed. What does that mean? It means to bring life your energy and ambition. Bring to life your goals, hopes and aspirations and on the way, don't forget to bring your work ethic. Bring focus, and effort.

Your drive, your willingness to grind for what you want, your passion, your purpose, your emphatic will to win. Bring life all of that energy and life will gladly match you pound for pound. Actually, I believe if you bring your will to succeed, life will match you double. Most certainly, one thing I experienced was if you go all out, you'll get more than what you asked for. Isn't that amazing? That's one of the greatest feelings in the world, if you ask me.

It's a pleasant surprise, a joyful occasion, and an extraordinary experience. When you planned to make 20 and instead got 40, it feels awesome. I remember working at Delta Sonic. It's a car care company. They specialize in interior and exterior detailing and cleaning of cars. I was a Delta Technician. My job was to make sure those cars got in and out in a hurry and were spotless.

We worked in a tip position job; we worked and dealt directly with customers every day. So, every day that I worked, I had the opportunity to come in broke and leave with a pocketful of money. I would go in and set a target. My target would be anywhere from $1 to $300.

I shot for just $1 on rainy days because when it rained or snowed we wouldn't get a lot of customers. For some reason the people thought that rain cleaned their car so they felt no need to come in and get a wash. Why get it washed when the rain will do it for you? lol. I shot for $300 on busy days.

The sun would be shinning and the weather would be nice between 40 and 60 degrees.

That's great weather for upstate New York during the end of the winter season. Everybody would pile in trying to get the salt off their car inside and out. They would pack the car wash and interior all day long from start to finish. Those were the days I would plan to work a double. 12-plus hours if I could. Actually I did that multiple times back to back. I even opened at 6 a.m. and left at close 10 p.m..

Those days, I was guaranteed $200 or more. Moral of the story: I went in with my seed (effort) and the earth (job) supplied double what I asked for or needed.

Here's another powerful quote I want to leave you with. "Those who fail to plan are planning to fail," Benjamin Franklin. Develop a plan. Come up with some short-range and long-range goals. Figure out what you want and don't want. Do not stop until you get it. Don't stop until you achieve it and never give up, ever. Because we already know winners never quit and quitters never win.

I believe in you. I believe in your brain power. I believe in your work ethic, and I believe in your inner potential. I believe you can and will succeed and achieve everything you put your mind to accomplish.

Use this book for a reference every year. Every time you need a boost of encouragement, a new idea or just a refresher. Never hesitate to share this book with family or friends. Spread the word. Spread the teachings. Share the information and wisdom. Use these principles and strategies time and time again. Be great, do great, live great.

Have faith, trust the process and overcome any obstacle, teacher, class, subject, friend, or test in your way. Say this with me:

"The best is yet to come.

Watch me work.

The best is yet to come.

I will be successful.

The best is yet to come.

I will go above and beyond to bring out the best in me."

Author Bio

Ariel is one of Central New York's top youth motivational speakers. He is a husband and father of two daughters; family is one of his top priorities. Ariel is also an author, entrepreneur and founder of Ariel Inspires LLC. He believes education is the key opportunity that helped him make it out of the harsh and challenging streets of

Syracuse, New York. Although he grew up in poverty with a single mother in a household of six, he took full advantage of education in order to transform his life. He went on to graduate with both his associates and bachelor's degrees and turned his passion of helping others into a business.

Traveling the world and impacting students is his dream job. His purpose in life is to help encourage and influence students all over the globe to be the best that they can be. Ariel achieves this by empowering students with the knowledge that they, too, can accomplish their wildest dreams through education and sheer determination. Ariel uses his most sought-after keynotes, workshops, and book to help transform students from good to great. He prepares students for college and also for entering the workforce.

Ariel is also the radio show host of his popular show, Prayer Session, on www.

blogtalkradio.com/prayersession. He uses his gift of speaking to pray for people in their time of need. Fashion is another one of his many talents, which he uses to put motivational and inspirational quotes on his signature clothing brand, Ari.

AUTHOR BIO

If this book has helped you, I invite you to leave a positive review of **Student Success Mindset** on Amazon.com

Made in the USA
Columbia, SC
22 November 2024